ALAN MOORE · HOW NOW!

T0159760

POETRY BY ALAN MOORE

Opia

ALAN MOORE

How Now!

Anvil Press Poetry

Published in 2010
by Anvil Press Poetry Ltd
Neptune House 70 Royal Hill London SE10 8RF
www.anvilpresspoetry.com

This book is published with financial assistance
from Arts Council England

Designed and set in Monotype Ehrhardt by Anvil
Printed and bound in Great Britain
by Hobbs the Printers Ltd

ISBN 978 0 85646 432 4

A catalogue record for this book
is available from the British Library

In memory of
EAMONN MOORE
(21.07.1929–13.09.1995)

O, let me not be mad, not mad, sweet heaven,
Keep me in temper: I would not be mad.
How now, are the horses ready?

– King Lear I.v

ACKNOWLEDGEMENTS

Acknowledgements are due to *Harvest* (Chinese Gospel Church of Dublin) and *Poetry Ireland Review* where some of these poems first appeared.

CONTENTS

Upper Park

The Rock of Cashel means we're nearly there.
A farmer with a load of hay is going slow in front of us.
"For the love of Jesus," Daddy grumbles.
"Control your tongue, Eamonn," Mammy tells him.
Straws in the wind. We shoot past the tractor.
"Gobshite," Daddy says.
"You'll kill us all," Mammy says.
We wave at the farmer. He smiles with his three teeth.

We gallop up the steps of Upper Park,
Past the otter and down the stairs.
The black kettle is where it was last year.
Granda puts down his *Cork Examiner*
And takes out his glass eye for us to see.
I find stamps in the drawer.
"Take them all boy," he says.

I climb the steps in the back yard, and cross the road to
       the dairy.
I bring back two bottles of milk.
Nana lets me put cream on my cornflakes.
She has kind eyes.
She never shouts at me.

She washes his shirts with a pink soap brick.
She stubs a bluebottle on the window.
It falls, its guts squeezed out beside its legs.
I hand her wooden pegs from a USA tin
And she hangs the shirts on the line.
A puddle grows beneath each dripping sleeve.

Glendoher

Our garden is a building site.
Bootprints on plasterboard.
A yellow glove reaching for help.
My brother wipes his snot moustache
And shakes his playpen bars.
Paint pots, all smiles.
The whirly line rotates then waits.

We're poor because the immersion is always on.
That's why we have to hide from the milkman.
Cora, our new baby, has no worries. She smiles all day.
Daddy tightens the nuts on Brian's bike,
His face like the Boston Strangler.
The clothes on the line let off steam.
"Get me the red pliers," Daddy says.

"Undress," the Gestapo officer tells Nina.
She strips and stands in silence with
Her back to us. He examines her clothes.
"What is he looking for?" I ask.
Both my parents have suddenly gone deaf.

Our blackamoor has sad frog eyes and a bulldog grimace.
Giant Haystacks has a headlock on Big Daddy.
The referee can't see as Haystacks hits Big Daddy's head.
"Why don't you go and play?" Daddy asks me.
"With who?"
"What about that specky-eyed git you hang round with?"
"Everybody is gone away for the bank holiday."
"Well stop arsing around," he says.

The rocking horse bares his white teeth.

A doll in tears, her leg amputated.
Torn newspapers. A destroyed lego house.
No life in Action Man's blue eyes.
"Tidy up" Mammy says.
I wish I could wiggle my nose like Samantha
Or have Jeannie tidy the room and say
"Is that all you require, Master?"
But I pick up the bricks myself.

Wind wolf-whistles down our chimney.
Brian, the twins and Cora are asleep.
Fionnuala counts monopoly money.
Margaret cuts out a dress pattern.
News at Ten dwindles to a dot.
The lights are out all over Glendoher.
I strike a match and watch its flare
Reduce this fat candle to tears.

I storm out of the house.
I stand outside Buglers imagining the warmth inside.
Daddy arrives and we declare a truce.
Ron Mael, immobile as a mime artist,
Massaging his keyboard, welcomes us home.

I find an injured thrush beside our swing.
I put him in a wheelbarrow and feed him milk-soaked bread.
But he is having none of it.
Next day, his dead eye stares at me.
I bury his feather-light stiff remains.
José hugs me and says: "Not cry."

A sunbeam, pure vermilion, spotlights the floor.
Daddy, tie loose, peers up from his crossword.
Pan's People dressed as air hostesses,
Dancing to *Typically Tropical*.

"Turn off that noise," he says.
"No wait," he says when Sue starts to unzip.
She volleys a beachball to Babs.
They frolic happily.
He frowns then clicks his Parker Pen again.

Glasnevin North

Jack Lynch looks down from every pole.
Mammy likes him because he comes from Cork.
Daddy says he should be taken out and shot.
I'm walking to the shops with Timothy.
He always looks sleepy.
"My father will give me the belt tonight," he says.
"What did you do? Poison his tea?"
"Nothing."
"Do his trousers not fall when he takes off his belt?"
"He has a special belt for hitting me.
He hangs it on the kitchen door."
"Oh."

Doug and Tony are both shot through the heart.
Merlin sends the bolts back to their crossbows.
"Are you not having any tea?" Mammy says.
"I'm not hungry," I say.
Although I am.

Cherry blossom petals shower my path.
Is it eight years since I lived here?
The daffodils all nod.
My Captain Scarlet wallpaper is gone.
The witch cottage is smothered by ivy.
Nettles nestle where I once feared to tread.

1973

Alvin Stardust beckons me with driving-gloved hand.
The microphone charmed into submission by his crooning.
Margaret in tears as Donny Osmond sings.
Daddy looks up from his paper and says:
"He looks as if he has constipation."

I lean over the green bridge rail and watch the Owendoher
Whisk away twigs and leaves and pieces of cardboard.
The rain belts down on Ballyroan Road.
I shelter in a hardware store –
With garden tools, lawn seed, daffodil bulbs.

A Triumph's walnut wood dashboard.
Tubular Bells by the leather-skirted gear stick.
Stacks of *The Exorcist* exude fresh ink.
In silver lamé robe behind the till in *Solar Sounds*
Gary Glitter looks shocked when I purchase *Aladdin Sane*.

We climb the round tower's steep stairs.
Dazzling white clouds gallop.
So easy to fall over the low rail and join the dead below.
So many there that once could smell and taste and see.
My heart jerk-drops on coffin ropes.

1967

A witch lives in the house by the school gates.
Margaret saw her sweeping with her witch broom.
Her dog barks all day long.
Maybe the dog's a child she put under a spell.
Maybe she even cooks and eats children.
So now I walk to school the other way.
I don't want to end up in her oven.

Mrs Gilboy smoothes the teapot cosy.
Jeremy clicks the train tracks together.
The engine starts a decade of the rosary.
The bruise beneath his fingernails is like a leak of ink.
"Sorry I dropped the grate," I say.
We watch Napoleon and Ilya defeat their evil enemies.
Get Smart is next.

Mother of pearl chalice in my rosette.
Jesus is inside me for the first time.
And he is not getting away without at least
One miracle. A giant Lego set.
A James Bond car with an ejector seat.

Heaven

My mammy blows her nose and waves bye bye.
I think the boy beside me didn't wipe his bum.
Mammy said Max died because he ate sand.
Now the thick dog is in heaven with God
And millions of angels. When I grow up
I want a dumper truck so I can drive
Through muck. And a Post Office Book
For my money. Then I will be happy.

Scent of honeysuckle.
Clouds move along on their assembly line.
Whitegate's paint pots are transmuted to gold.
A butterfly rollercoasters among the nasturtiums.
The dandelions sway like a gospel choir.
Sometimes I want the world to end, but not today.
I hope heaven will be like this.

Teachers

1

He lifts Ciarán's tiny hurley for all to see.
Everyone laughs except Ciarán and me.
I don't like this teacher.
He smells like an ashtray.
And he spits when he speaks.

2

I ask my new teacher why "answer" has a "w".
There is no need for it.
He says it is an Anglo-Saxon word.
We can't change every book in the whole world.
He sends me to the Principal to get more chalk.
I pretend to smoke one as I walk back.
He swoops his cane missing my bum and says: "Now run
    along."
So I run like Lassie after eating
Meaty chunks of Pedigree Chum.

3

He drags me to the waiting room.
The clock buzzes like a trapped fly.
"Put out your hand," he says. *Swoop. Swoop.*
"The other one," he says. *Swoop. Swoop.*
James Connolly seems satisfied.
Patrick Pearse looks away.

Daddy

He leans down to kiss me and something squeaks.
He lifts the sheet and thirteen pairs
Of teddy eyes look back at him in fear.
"Why have you all of these in here?"
"I'm minding them," I say.
I wish he was always nice as he is now.
I can't believe he is the same Daddy who said
This morning at breakfast: "You shut your trap."
Then his face looked like Captain Black.

Drizzle flattens the weeds in our garden.
The Biafrans have big bellies because they are starving.
Daddy's belly is big from beer.
He asks me why I have such a long face.
I tell him Robin will be boiled in oil.
"Don't be stupid. He has to be alive
For next week's episode," he says.
He gives me a fat pen with buttons for every colour.

Rain tap-dances on the roof of Daddy's Morris.
A Chipperfield's circus truck in my hand.
I smell the new red seats and watch the drops
Join up and grow as they wash the window.
The two giraffes look out of their blue box.
I want to cry but I do not know why.

Drops on the washing line queue up to fall.
Daddy reads his paper.
I read my book about the moon mission.
"Why did they blow up the Pillar?"
"Because Nelson was a great man."
In the command module, a pack of food floats free.
"Are they going to build it again?"

"No."
"Does that mean I can't go to the top?"
"Yes."

Glass of Champagne booms from fridge-sized speakers.
Strobe lights slow down an embracing couple.
Their frog-tongues kiss.
His hands knead her bum cheeks.
Daddy waits up with a face like the anti-Christ.
"Where's that trollop sister of yours?"

I sit in a tube train with David and Tracy.
Across from us sits Mammy from *Gone With the Wind*,
Complete with head hankie. We're stopped.
An Australian backpacker with damp armpits
Hangs from a strap, smiles at his Japanese girlfriend.
Sweat pearls on her forehead. A sudden jolt,
And we lurch off. A welcome breeze.
The man in the suit resumes his crossword.

"Will you read this?"
After the news.
When I finish reading my magazine.
After I cut the grass.
After I wash my hands.
When we come home from mass.
When you eat your carrots.
After my swim.
When you pick up your toys and put them all away.
When you tidy up your jigsaw.
When I lose thirty pounds.
When I finish writing these words.
When I scan my photos.
One day. Next week. Next year. Not now.

Chorley

The flaps groan down. The wheels thump into position.
Washing lines welcome us to Liverpool.
Reverse thrusters thunder.
We sit in Uncle Bert's Austin Cambridge.
Daddy says the roads are a real pleasure
Compared to the lunar landscape at home.
Aunt Monica asks me in a John Lennon voice:
"Want some pop, love?"

The front door bangs. Uncle Bert and Daddy
Fall in with arms on each other's shoulders.
Bert has hiccups. Daddy a stupid smile.
Aunt Monica shouts from upstairs:
"Don't waste your time looking for the whiskey.
It's under lock and key." Uncle Bert groans:
"Can't a man have a drink in his own house?"

Daddy gives Mammy her present.
A leather bag. Her eyes are like the Hood.
She beats him on the head with it.
We sit at the top of the stairs hearing them fight.
Mammy stomps past and starts to pack her case.
"Don't go, Mammy," Fionnuala bawls.

Sunday

Grey three piece suite and granite fireplace.
Whiskey smell from the press.
I empty the hoover's grey candy floss.
A blonde in a towel admired by a huzzar.
George Best smiles from his new red Jaguar.

I spray a wasp with Mr Sheen.
He drones down like a damaged fighter plane
Into the fluff beneath the net curtain.
He spins like a skater for one minute then stops.
His sting moves in and out.
His antennae move less and less.
His pincer mouth tries to vomit his proboscis.
His wings give one final flourish.
His legs stiffen.

The church of the Holy Spirit is an upright vacuum cleaner,
Sucking everyone in. It smells of Brut and cigarettes.
The gold-piped organ moans.
Dust motes gyrate in a shaft of sunlight.
Preceded by four smirking altar boys, the priest arrives.
"Stop fidgeting," Daddy tells me.
A toddler wails and kicks as she is carried off.
Mary looks to heaven behind ranks of candles.
The choir drowns us in the Hallelujah chorus.

A Starfighter hangs by two threads from my ceiling.
Hissing saucepans in the kitchen.
Margaret bashes the spuds.
Daddy carves the roast beef.
The cat observes from the kitchen window,
Licking her face with a single tongue sweep.

Cobh

We ease out of Heuston, past stacks of old sleepers
And patches of oil-stained gravel.
Pylons perform aerobics in the fields.
A dog rounds up his scattered flock.
A combine harvester excretes hay bricks.
Alyssum overflows from small station windows.
The engine utters its assurances.
The wheels crack jokes with the ecstatic track.

We burn our bums on the red hot leather
Of Uncle Mick's grey Anglia.
He hands us two ice cream wafers.
Mine dribbles down my arm.
"Dare's a tissue in dare," he says
Opening the glove compartment.
Thinking he said "Just throw it there," I do.
"What did you do *dat* for?"
"You told me to."
He does not go mental.
"We'll clean it up when we get home."

A cloud like a rearing white horse.
The beach bin overflows: ice pop wrappers and Fanta cans.
Trigger-happy snipers take aim at ducks.
Toy windmills whirr as Dr Hook whimpers.
Dodgems headbutt and squeal, their tails sparking.
The waves shampoo seaweed tresses.
I walk out into the water.
I stand on shifting sand.
Briny fingers surround my throat.

Friends

Trudi, his Yorkshire terrier, patters toward me
And vibrates on my shin.
Big Tom grins from behind the bowl of fruit.
We listen to *Ride of the Valkyries*
And the Eleventh Panzer Grenadiers.
After, we walk down to the Yellow House.
Heads crouch over chess boards.
The ceiling overcast with cigar smoke.

On the mantel beside the crucifix:
Duphalac and Milk of Magnesia.
His mouth is now a flap of flesh.
Rosary beads hang from his blackened thumbs.
God knows how many worms now thrive inside those hands.
Hands that could tell counterfeit notes.
Hands that lifted a happy baby me.

She brushes blusher on her cheeks,
Applies her mascara,
Then pouts at her scarlet-lipped reflection.
She puts on her blue teddy bear fur coat.
Tombstones surround the small group of mourners.
The coffin clunks into its resting place.

Christian Brothers

One angel feather in the sky.
A parliament of crows debates.
I gulp in nicotine outside the gates.
Two seagulls stuka-dive a crust
Creating a snowstorm of crumbs.

Blue holes in the sky's grey jumper.
A crowd studies the eyes of a dead cat.
Nylon blue washing line around its neck.
Milk-white fangs protruding above its gums.
"Ever seen a cat with a banger up its arse?" says Flynn.
A gauntlet of moss grips the drainpipe's throat.
The school door whinges about its hinges.

Ejaculate-grey sky. Swaying dock weeds.
A paper plane squadron surrounds the waste basket
Like sperm crowding an egg. The door darkens.
With two quick finger snaps, Modo restores order.
His Mussolini eyes scan for signs of dissent.
He sweeps out of the room leaving a smell
Of sweat and smoke. The clock purrs.

Our boots imprint the muddy battleground.
Clatter of football studs on the parquet.
Happy ache in our joints as we troop home
With our sports bags, bicycle chains clicking.
A Volkswagen's brake lights
Glare like rubies in the drizzle.

Hail popcorns off the exam hall's steel roof.
A non-rickety desk. Unload biros, tippex.
A fly patrols above our heads.
Dan's tartan-striped half-mast trousers
Shake as he scratches his answer.
A sunbeam shines his Doc Martens.

Infatuations

1

A hollow's leaves, like cornflakes in a bowl.
The clouds are spurts of shaving cream.
The strange beauty of her grey gabardine.
She strokes her strawberry blonde hair
And stoops to tie her lace.

My heart hovers on a soft air cushion.
Rising, she shifts her shoulder strap and strides,
Schoolbag bouncing against her hip.
O Lord, please let me be a corpuscle
In her bloodstream for just one day.

Pansies observe me with binoculars.
Her aura as she walks to work.
She stretches to refill the display of Aeros.
Her face turns tomato when she sees me.
Now say something. Anything.

2

Drizzle sizzles on my Honda's exhaust.
Who is this clone of Nastassja Kinski?
Her cigarette smoke spirals vertically.
Her smile pummels my heart into jelly.

3

Both fists in her blue windcheater.
Sweet smile on her perfect white teeth.
Twirling gold hair behind her ear.
Pizza by candlelight.
Wine bottle like a howitzer,
A smoke kiss blowing from its lips.
My brain unravels as the drink invades.
Why do I feel so unworthy?

Summer

I grip the scythe's smooth horns and cut
The legs from under the long grass.
Cuckoospit nests collapse as I advance like Death.
A frog leaps clear of my destructive arc.
As I sharpen the blade
I slide my thumb along its edge.
A scarlet drop swells in the hinge of skin.
An earthworm twists beneath the vermicelli roots.

The sun illumines gauzy clouds.
The light toys with my fork as I shovel
Fried eggs and toast into my mouth.
I try to reconstruct my movements for last night.
I must have drunk at least ten pints.
Seagulls bicker. Motorbike snarl.
Will someone shut that door?

Pink sweetpea spires in Avenue Flanders.
Foxgloves like stilled sleigh-bells.
The privet leaves shimmy
Like Donna Summer singing *I Feel Love*.

A perfect day: blue sky, milk haze;
Sunglasses and ultraviolet rays.
The lavender luxuriates:
The grass stems wave their plaits.
A bee struggles to get his legs over
The flushed, surprised, clover.

Girlfriend

Orange bubbles coalesce on the wall.
Five girls, arms linked, kick up their heels
And hip-swivel to *Make Me Smile*.
At the song's pause, they become mannequins
Then come to life again when the chords sound.
We move to *Wide-Eyed and Legless*.

Sunsilk in my nostrils.
Schubert's E flat trio.
We taste each other's tongues and watch
Barry Lyndon bully Lord Bullingdon.
My fingers panzer into her Ardennes.
Beneath our seat, a lepidopterist's heaven.

Navan

Cotton tufts on sky's shaving cuts.
Unshuttering of shops in Trimgate Street.
The caged ultra-violet tube in the butcher's
Window displays its insect carcasses.
Wasps orbit every rubbish bin.

Jaws eats up all the carousel spaces.
My brush scoots beneath the Radion shelves
Extracting liquorice banana skins,
A fungus-bearded apple core.
With five biros in his white breast pocket,
My boss's boss thinks he can inspire me.
He gives me a Dick Nixon grin as I stack spuds.
"Well done. You're doing a fantastic job."
I want to say: *Silence, Sirrah!*
You beastly knave! Know you no reverence?

A wall of heat. Bluebottle thoraxes dazzle.
An open grave of rotting bananas.
Traders pack up their stalls,
Place their plastic-wrapped suits in Hi-Ace vans.
A Cape apple tray somersaults across the square.
Red Hurley's tannoy voice stops abruptly.
Crows' cawed applause.
The evening sky, a glowing horizontal slit,
A sword cooling in its mould.

The checkout girls gossip and paint their nails.
White clouds appear in my bucket
Water when I add the disinfectant.
I move my mop like a mine detector.

Tiles gleam in the heat haze.
I wipe the window squeaky clean.

I smoke with my new pal,
My upturned dreadlocked mop.
We watch the flies above the skip,
Re-enacting the Battle of Britain.

On Academy Street, a bee cuffs me.
Past fresh wood-shaving smells to the Mollies,
Where poppies form a Soviet parade.
A red admiral inspects the thistles.
Children frolic in the spangled river.
A black spaniel drags a wake cape,
Emitting earnest ruffs.
My muscles ache after a brutal day.
Gunsmoke wisps from my opened Harp bottle.
I crease the cap into a clam. And slug.

The tarmac smokes, ignoring tears of joy:
Drops on shrink-wrapped pink toilet rolls.
Only someone who knows *King Lear* by heart,
With a bionic ear, could hear Oswald's *Untimely death!*
When Edgar runs him through as *I Am the Walrus*
    concludes.
An old dear smiles with lipstick-stained dentures.
Why wear a fur coat in July?
Her poodle yelps. Apple scent in the freezer aisle.
Beautiful Noise cedes to *Trouble with a Capital T.*

Family Time

Slicing tomatoes on the chopping board, Mammy asks me:
"Will you feed those kittens?"
They look at me imploringly, tails vibrating.
One rubs his nose against my shoe, idling his starved engine.
I pour the milk into a Denny's dish and watch
Their tongues dab at the calcium-enriched goodness.
A jinny jo on the satin surface
Fails to disturb their tripartite lapping.

Daddy sits on the bed, surrounded by his bills.
"What the fuck do *you* want?" he says.
I see fear in his bloodshot eyes.
"Nothing," I say as he impales
Final demands on a hanger.
 "Just go," he says, avoiding any further eye contact.
A distant ice cream van tinkles *The Sting*.

Approaching the front door, I hear the usual uproar.
"I'm not doing it, and that's final."
"Well fuck you too."
A raucous crash, a slamming door.
Mammy sits gazing at a broken jar,
The sugar-frosting on the floor.
"Your dinner is in the oven."
Fionnuala sucks a long spaghetti string.

In Uniform

I wake in a cold sweat.
The dread of being conscious in my grave,
Surrounded by foul-smelling presences.
Grey steel bedside locker.
Each soldier's boots beneath his bed.
Sunlight on a brass belt buckle.
A tunic sways like a body on a gibbet.

Flamingo sky. Boots clunk in unison.
We're on parade in Longford barracks square.
SC moves like R2D2, salutes and bleeps.
"Are you okay?" Matt says.
Truth is, only in a Charles Manson kind of way.
I want to burn this place.
I want no one to know it ever existed.

A jet incises cloudless sky.
Butterflies waltz with the poppies.
Puff of cordite. Spent brass glitters.
Bullets thumping the silhouettes.
Were I to go mental with my Gustaf
The body count would be significant.
I wipe my brow.

Leaving Certificate

Physics by the Christian Brothers weighs down my bag.
I gravitate homeward past the pig farm's foul stench.
I hear their squeals as they compete for the ideal trough
    position.
A Superquinn bag tries to extricate itself from thorns.
The *Coronation Street* theme welcomes me.
I escape to study and sane Radio Three.

Mozart's final piano concerto, the twenty-seventh in B flat.
Already he had composed enough for twenty.
Heart-enclosed boyfriend names in *Scothscéalta* margins.
The cat snores by the fire, one ear twitching,
Kittens asleep between her outstretched paws.
Daddy is reading *Private Eye*.

Fares, please!

What colour is the 15B?
A mix of orange sand, ochre and French mustard.
What accessories does it wear?
It drips with strings of radiant raindrops.
Fragrance?
Diesel.
How does it sound?
It grunts and groans. It shrieks and moans. It sighs.
How does it feel?
Its seats' innards exposed by multiple burn holes,
It trembles at the traffic lights.
Are you in love with it?
No comment.

The conductor dials his machine
And slides the coins into his leather bag.
The upper deck is jabbed by bare-knuckled
Branches as we shudder toward An Lár.
Wipe the steamed-up window and you will see schoolboys
Like mountaineers imprinting the fresh snow.

Alcohol and Me

A squad of pints standing to attention.
Guinness like oil in the spill trays.
Behind, a row of teats:
Paddy, Huzzar, Teachers.
Pizzicato polka in the white urinal.
I ease into brain dead oblivion.

I lie on newspapers on black floorboards.
My brain is a roulette wheel ball.
My forehead feels like one enormous bruise.
Burger bits rise like islands in the puke river
That meanders from my shirt to the floor.
Light streams through the window.
Where is this place?
I struggle to my feet like an injured insect.
I heave into the kitchen sink.
Why do I poison my own well?
I need to know.

My flexi-key's red eye expires.
Pete puffs his pipe and says "Good luck."
A row of icicles like t. rex teeth.
I squeeze inside and find a stool beside the hearth.
A pint is put in front of me.
A mocking voice: "Behold the bard! Seat thee!"

I queue for fish and chips.
Demons hiss happily as spuds arrive in oil.
My brain floats free within my skull.
Coins down the drain as I headbutt the kerb.

Sun shines a briefcase lock.
"You were knotty-eyed in Railway last night."
"Was I? I don't remember anything!"
The lock un-clicks.

Blue smoke from the express train dissipates.
My brain wet with alcohol poisoning.
Like a punch-drunk boxer, I watch sunlight
Brighten then shade the Magazine Fort walls.
I feel for the pear tree: with ivy sleeves rolled up,
Its bare knuckles have dodged and weaved all day,
Twisting to avoid heaven's attention.

Andy to drug addict in the pokey:
There are many reasons to get loaded.
It's usually because you hate your life.
Starlings swirl like a gladiator net.
Trees exercise in ivy legwarmers.
I trudge through the wet sand,
Cheeks stung by rain. Speckled pebbles,
Broken blue blades of mussel shells.
Is any of this getting through, ASSHOLE?

Belfield

Fingers frozen inside my gloves.
I chain the wheel, lock my helmet,
And join the restaurant queue.
A Goth girl looks adoringly at her partner.
His hand guards her leather-skirted behind.
Warm smell of scrambled eggs on toast.
I trickle coins to the till lady's hand.

Metaphysics Exam. I lock my car
And see the keys still in the ignition,
The throbbing engine, taunting me.
I phone Daddy. Expecting a tirade.
He does not mock.
I emerge after three long hours.
He hands the keys to me.

Civil Service

My boss shows me to the Sorting Office.
His breath reeks of whiskey.
A postman deals letters to open-mouthed sacks.
"You're only a bollix, Murphy," he says.
"Who is he talking to?" I ask.
"Never mind," my boss says.

The lift dings at the Parcel Post.
I'm left with Albert and Eddie.
At five we eat vinegared chips in the canteen.
"Want to join us in the North Star?"
The crimson sun attains oblivion.

The waitress reveals a nipple
As she bows to take my order.
She smiles and looks me in the eye
For longer than necessary.
But sadly this can never be.
No one ever sees my soul's skeletons.
Except the one who holds the key. That's me.

The smoky smell of files.
I read my World War II in the canteen.
The typists pour the tea.
I think of my Honda in the car park below.
Tonight I'll go to Portmarnock and watch
Waves lather, rinse and repeat, as necessary.

A curtain of rain sweeps across Elm Park.
Mick sits in his wheelchair, thigh stump cut short
Above the knee. Somehow he is happy.
He strips the cellophane from a bottle of Lucozade.
A flock of bubbles ascends in the glass.

"Want some?" he asks by raising his eyebrows.
I wave that I do not.

Seagulls scour the blue sky above Dublin Castle.
A tree has almost finished its striptease:
Only one modest leaf remains.
A biker crowns himself with his helmet.
His throttle-twist releases a lilac genie.
With fresh baguette for jousting lance
He steers past the amazed windscreens.

A girl arrives red-faced and plonks her bag beside her desk.
My boss tells me to say: *Was disponer a car-owner?*
Little Peter drops a file on my desk.
He smiles with moist blue eyes,
Then shuffles off with his trolley.
Dennis writes poems about cancer and skulls.
His handwriting looks like barbed wire.

The wipers cannot cope with floods of tears.
I park in a VISITOR space.
Cardinal red cathedral analysis books,
Bank statements and invoice folders.
Outside, a forklift twists and turns.
"How is it going?" asks the owner.
"Several discrepancies," I say.
The smile forsakes his face.
He twists his wedding ring.

A smell of glue in our brand new office.
Stacked chairs in the canteen
Still wrapped in polythene.
Yellow fluff moults from the carpet.
Christmas lights in neighbours' windows.

Save Your Love on the stereo
As I overtake a tractor.
Not good when ice cannot be seen.
My world turns upside down:
The windscreen sprinkles me.
The engine hisses me as I crawl out.
The frosted grass, so delicate!
How come I've never noticed it?

A few snowflakes settle on a windscreen
And urge their fellows to join them.
Millions respond,
And now the white wisps fill the air,
Following one another in freefall,
Tumbling around and down.

Casimir Road

Ivy on the breeze wall resists arrest.
Scent of Old Spice in the bathroom.
The landing's dusty May altar:
The Blessed Virgin standing on a snake,
Plastic pink roses in a vase,
The drawers stuffed with mass cards,
A rosary coiled in its silk-lined box.

The pantry's red floor tiles. Lubricant oil.
A bulb wearing a dust toupée.
Traveller's Joy tobacco tins containing tacks,
Brass screws, and dust-furred curtain hooks.
The toolbox innards on display:
A family of screwdrivers, assorted pliers,
Claw hook hammers, fuses, measuring tape.
Rust-spotted saw and its hacksaw sibling.

I see him through tobacco haze,
Sitting on the storage heater,
Scorching his pipe bowl with his flame thrower.
He stoop-shuffles to the kitchen, punctures
Sausages with a fork and lays them on the grill.
The tap nozzle dangles its drop over the sink.
The fridge pontificates in the corner.

A tea towel trapezes on the washing line.
I chew my blackened toast.
"Have you given up mass altogether?" he says.
"It means nothing to me," I say.
He dons his overcoat and black beret,
Breathing like Darth Vader.
The letter-box flaps as the door closes.
I like his honesty.

The way his Cortina expectorates
In unison with him.

Mirage pools on Casimir Road.
Red armchairs beside the coal-effect fire.
The frigging mantel clock, the silver cigar box.
The brass urn on the grey doily.
Vulture jumper and purple corduroys.
She finishes her masters on *la Boétie*.
Her Gauloise butts in the ashtray,
A smouldering rail disaster . . .
Haunch hug on my growling Honda.
In the Greyhound, a Pacman gobbles up the dots.
A scrum of coats at the stairpost.
Ash lips on mine.

Grass clipping scent. It's almost noon.
Grandfather clock tuts to itself.
On the floor a red sock, a sweaty turquoise top.
Taps fill the bath with a gush of applause.
I listen to *Brain Damage* by Pink Floyd.
A froth of iridescent bubbles grows.
I settle myself in the cackling brew.
 "You want me to join you?"

Ash sky. I gaze from the bedroom window.
Casimir Road under assault by snow.
The flakes descend erratically and merge
With others that control the lilac verge.
The cars are now white humps by the roadside.
It's famine for the gawking crows. They hide
In their nests high above snow-wigged gravestones:
Rows of freshly made beds for weary bones.
I trepanate my egg and drink my tea.
Grandad scans the death list, coughing hoarsely.

Hell

The Bourbon sun intoxicates the sea.
Stale Smithwicks, exorcised from me,
Showers ditch flames of Lucifer.
Gauloise wisps towards the voyeur stars.
She rubs herself with fevered urgency.

Rain-polished cobbles of Place des Abbesses.
The waiter wipes off the table, refills my cup.
A street cleaner manouvres his sprinkling machine.
I watch the leaves curtsey and then gavotte.
I manufacture snow with a beer mat.

Matrimony

I welcome the cool breeze
As we arrive at Lewisham,
Holding hands as young lovers should.
Black cab to Breakspears Road.
The dandelions fold up their parasols.
A black cat tip-toes on the moss-patched wall,
Pauses and stares into my soul:
Where *Crazy For You* plays repeatedly.

    When you stand at the rail of the altar
    And wait for your bride to arrive,
    The butterflies begin to take off within
    And it's good to be alive.

I am now an exam-passing robot.
When I get home, our child is in her cot.
Five years of cohabitation with me.
Your dreams never conjured such misery.
Silent treatment, put-downs, mental abuse.
You watch your *Eastenders*, I watch the news.
No doubt I am a psychiatric case.
Sorry for wiping the smile off your face.

    When you place your ring on her finger
    And she puts hers on yours,
    You want the moment to linger
    You do not think of divorce.

Fellow Poet

A sea of white and yellow flags:
A million here to see the white-haired man.
His jet drones low above the cheering mass.
A day of hymns and smiles,
Hearing about the laugh of Christ.
He ploughs the happy throng with his open top van,
Then ascends to heaven again,
Having relit the candles in our souls.

Knocklyon

His stomach protrudes from
His beige waist-length jacket
(The uniform for recently retired
Curmudgeons with anger issues).
His grey leather slip-ons patting
The harsh concrete, he winces as
He bends, straining to hear.

What words pass between us?
I struggle to recall a phrase.
No doubt we dwelt upon
The issues of the day:
The war in Bosnia,
Political incompetence,
His grandchildren's summer visit.

He grips my sleeve as we pass Superquinn,
Where wind stirs bank machine receipts,
And turns to me, others' needs written on
His face. "What is it?" I venture,
As if expecting some profound reply. "Nothing."
He knew. But how was I to know
That this would be our last walk in fresh air?

Tenerife

for Sean Lennon

O Aeropuerto Reina Sofia
You breathe warm air
On me
And kiss
My soul to life again.

Whether it is the sand in your ashtrays
Or the glittering trolley snake, I cannot say:
All I know is that as we leave the terminal,
My life moves from monochrome to colour.
I am alive, and the stars are my friends.

O luminescent bougainvillea! O parasails!
O models in your day-glo pink swimsuits!
O surging surf, washing each grain!
Make me like this blue sky:
Wiped clean, and whole again.

Not Now

Ay, every inch a king! – KING LEAR IV.vi

Oranges heaped like cannonballs.
The room smells like a flower shop.
Bananas curved in foetal sleep.
We are all here: a farewell gathering.
He clutches the blanket like a praying mantis.
His temple vein flickers.

Frost stubble on his jaw. Ketosis smell.
He shuffles in his new slippers,
Holding the dripstand like a staff,
Pursued by kitten squeals.
His face resembles a Belsen inmate.
He stares at me. He does not know my face.

A nurse pulls the curtain, adjusts the drip
That tunnels into his yellow–mauve hand.
Mam takes the tissue from his claw,
Then smoothes his crown's last hairs.
I think of his small kindnesses:
Fizzing arclight – as my truck is welded.
His tears and laughter at the Diddymen.
His arsenal of ultimate put-downs:
Half-wit. Cretin. Apprentice gravedigger.
He stares at me. He does not know my face.

Behind Buglers, ants teem from footpath cracks.
A puffball cloud swells on its dark grey base.
A white poodle with tear-stained eyes pats past.
Daddy, you once told me how you were so
Afraid to hear your father vomit on
The stairs and see no evidence the next morning.
I hope he has explained himself.

Kilmainham

The rain types its latest novel.
I sit surrounded by my unpacked things.
A train shudders the double-glazed window
As it jackhammers thirty feet below.
Streetlights ignite in red then dim to pale orange.
The Phoenix Park is a black void.
Witness of my Harold's Cross years,
My TV says: *Don't look at me, buddy.*

Shopping trolley with a mind of its own.
Roasting chickens.
The look in a dead herring's eye.
Penile deodorants. A choice of panty pads.
Freckled bananas on their grassy knoll.
Love Is All Around Me persists inside
My brain as I carry my beer cans home.
Clouds flex above the still canal.
A pair of plastic bags begins to jitterbug.

A white cloud levitates above the park.
The pear tree has downloaded on the lawn.
One leaf wriggles, the others remain still.
Rust infects the chestnut spike husks.
I pour a can of ice-cold beer
And watch Kelly tell Sipowicz: "That guy is *wrong*."
Next door's burglar alarm tests my patience.
Neons patrol their world. God offers me the moon:
A soluble antacid pill, dissolved in clouds.

When finished my abdominals,
I sweat it out at the bench press.
The ghettoblaster thumps the floor:

I know there's something going on.
Females in skintight leotards step up
And back repeatedly. The instructress
Sucks her bottle's crenellated pink straw.
My hormones urge that I impregnate her:
She is capable of bearing many children.
But I am one among competing males.
I beat up the punch bag, let loose my rage.

Murderous screams from next door's apartment.
Their headboard taps a morse code on my wall.
Outside, blackened branch fingers reach to snuff the stars.
Headlights hiss through a film of snow.
I see my father in his grave, gritting his teeth,
His hair grown like unravelled twine.

Evil

Pub closing time, caught on CCTV:
A youth knife-poked seven times in the back,
Foetal on a blanket of blood.
The assassin's face hidden by his hood.

There is the violence of sheer terror:
The face doused in a barrel of water.
The beating with nail-studded baseball bats.
The neck-snap as the trap-door opens wide.

A child lies on a sack sucking
Its dead mother's nipple.
Calf eyelashes stare death right in the face.
Flies jostle for the best places.

And there is the violence of silence:
The tension-filled culture of mind-control,
The fear that makes every heaven a hell.
The violence you have mastered so well.

An audience of smirking skulls.
Alone in the spotlight, the smallest skull,
Cranial plates unjoined.
The entry point between the eyes.

You rarely get to see people being killed,
But you can get lucky. I've got some real gems.
I'm always ready to press RECORD when I hear:
Some viewers may find these scenes disturbing.

The hands that lead the toddler through the shopping mall.
The injection from your calm family doctor.
The guillotine's officious swish.
The way the jet wing dips, as it makes its final turn.

The Answer

I always looked for the answer outside myself:
I wanted the miracle drug, the poem, the painting,
The music, the place, the experience, something
That would finally fix me and once and for all
Irretrievably, irrevocably, make me whole.
I looked everywhere except within.

But when I did, I smelt my sin.

Dave

I cannot believe I'm smelling the incense
As Anne places a daffodil on your coffin.
The priest holds up your hiking boots for all to see.
One year ago, outside Nutgrove Tesco I asked:
"What's with the baseball cap?"
"It's the big C. I'm on chemo," you said.
Now you've climbed clear
Can you give a brief talk on life beyond?

What's it all about, Dave?
The chalk white sky gives no answer.
Is it a summer evening at the Pav,
Candyfloss clouds nibbled by sun?
If life is everywhere, why doubt it will persist?
I ignore the cherry blossom petals on my car roof.
But how can I avoid the miles of daffodils on the by-pass,
Sunlight hopping off my windscreen?

Fun

You are not here, but if you were,
Blown candle flames would quiver and expire,
The TV screen would beep digitally,
And fat balloons would burst with joy.

Your friends would celebrate your winning goal:
I'd squeeze you until you said *Let me GO!*
Later, I'd look upon your sleeping face
And watch your chest's light fall and rise.

Instead, I hear dark clouds mutter
As they water the flowers on your grave,
Washing this smooth black rectangle,
Your birth date in gold lettering.

My insides have been hollowed out;
My organs have been harvested;
Like this sodden toy bear, I'm beyond numb:
I've been struck deaf, and blind, and dumb.

You are not here, but if you were,
I'd learn to listen to your pain:
I'd look into your eager eyes, my son,
And say: *Come on. Let's have some fun.*

Sunlight

Showgirl palm trees toss their plumed heads.
Parasails trail thread tentacles.
Hot lunar sand between my toes.
Ant traffic between the floor tiles.
On the stone stairs, a piece of chewing gum,
White as a frozen embryo.

A jet twinkles above.
Eamonn stuffs melon in his mouth, screams for his cup.
Squashed mosquito in St Augustine's *Confessions*.
"You look like a homeless person," Tracy tells me.
Swifts skitter in the eaves.
Eamonn asleep like a praying Muslim.

Pot Black

I

Contrails,
Their long skid marks
Left by miscues
On God's
Snooker table.

God stands,
Relaxes his
Shoulders, then bends
To aim
For this long pot.

The pink
Sun drops into
The horizon's pocket.
The moon's
Cue ball returns.

2

He's decided to go for it.
It could be a frame-winning chance.
My word!
It wobbled for a while but it's gone in.
He's at his most dangerous now.
A simple black to leave Jimmy needing snookers.
He's missed!
But that's what happens when you're in the Crucible final.
I don't think anything is on except this cut to the middle pocket.
It's in!
Now can the former champion clear up?

Now

The glass is already broken.
— BUDDHIST FIRST NOBLE TRUTH

Acacia leaves shade me.
The grass is cool beneath my feet.
I sit on a white chair beside the pool.
A fat boy plunges in, to shrieks and squeals.
The sky has only one smear of suncream.
Tracy's goggles lie at my feet.
The leprechaun on her pen smirks at me.
A fly lands on my arm to rub his hands.
A two year old with chocolate beard
Says to her dad: "I didn't eat any."

I climb to our apartment door
And look over the terracotta tiles
To where a speedboat carves a white scratchmark.
A biplane drones above freshly-baked cliffs
Pursued by its banner: BEBE SUMO.
Convolvulus petals have closed.
Faint stars appear above the orange glow.
The sprinklers cannot drown out the crickets.
The moon drapes its long veil on the calm sea.
A hummingbird buzzes past our balcony box.

My car has been resprayed with frost.
I pour warm water on the glittering windscreen,
Dissolving fronds and Van Gogh swirls.
The engine splutters and resuscitates.
A jet like a slowly ascending flare.
Mauve clouds on peach background.
A hundred fuming car engines.

A hundred pairs of demon eyes.
A man massages with an electric razor.
A wise Buddha sucks his soother.

Like Hueys over Vietnam,
My toothbrush wages war on plaque and cavities.
I spit and wipe my rabid mouth.
I think of these teeth smiling in the grave
Their last fresh breath reserved for the cold earth.
My heart a happy meal for rice-grain worms.
My empty skull – the brain long-since melted –
Finally free of its incessant thoughts.
Finally able to relax and smile.

The cash machine hiding behind the door.
Aroma of grilled sausages. Heaped golden delicious.
A sultry stare. *Tips To Drive Your Man Wild.*
The mad-eyed blonde takes my ninety eight cents.
"Do you want a receipt for that?"
The scanner's droid-like beeps.
The till shuts up its motor mouth again.

The garden shed has become a sauna.
I sit on an inflatable armchair.
And just observe.
The satellite dish shadow grows longer.
Red spider mites patrol the sill.
A pink rose trembles in its stalk.
Plates placed on an outdoor table.
A stern voice to a child.
"No, I said NO."

Wind hums and haws. The tree head-bangs alone.
The magpie on the fence steadies himself,
Smoothes his ruffled feathers.

A drop falls from the eave in a flash of brilliance.
The grey curtain descends again.
The wheelie bin meditates by the door.
A hoarse rumble. Window sprinkle.
The silence changes to a carwash roar.

The willow weeps into the pond.
Mallards patrol in search of crumbs.
Jugglers exchange tenpins.
Mushrooms mass between the trunk's exposed roots.
Maple leaves trail like dinosaur footprints.

The four-wheel drive convoy departs.
The violin imparts a brief moment of empathy –
An interlude to be, briefly, stress-free.
Where have you hid the pearl that is your soul?
Futile to suppress the urge to blossom.
It's time to effloresce, to incandesce.

I built a wall of books around myself;
Sentries protect my soul on every shelf.
The inner sanctum wall is ten feet thick:
No light ever reaches its leaden brick.
Alone I sit in my black citadel;
I don't fear death: I'm already in hell.
I don't recall when my mind seized control –
When fear's black flag was raised over my soul.
The time has come to leave this place:
To surrender to light and truth and grace.

Pursing his lips, Eamonn blows his bubbles:
A sequence of sun-struck transparent spheres,
Lilac-tinted, in various sizes,
They escalate towards the pebble dash
Where mica mirrors constellate

To guide each fragile orb towards its fate.
There their perfection ends. They crash
Back to oblivion. No surprises.
They leave a stain of tears,
Their last remains. No more troubles.

Happy Days

Happiness is a warm gun – JOHN LENNON

1

Mammy tells me "Just read your book."
I'm sick of reading *Captain Cook*.
The rain has made a lake in our garden.
I hope some swans land there.
I feel sorry for John Tracy,
All alone in Thunderbird 5.
Do the Tracys have rows like us?
Who cooks dinners?
Who irons their uniforms?
Jeff could marry Lady Penelope.
Then they'd all be happy.

2

The cherry blossom trees
Are happy young bridesmaids:
They lean together in the breeze,
Petals flying from their braids.

When I quietly eat my Frosties
Aware of my character flaws
I hear the magpies' congratulations
And the frying pan's applause.

Oblivion

Gorse-coloured scabs on the tombstones.
An urn spray-painted with lime-green algae.
I know that my Redeemer liveth worn away.
In the aisle of yews, a gravedigger greets me:
"All right, Al? How's your love life?"
A minefield of rust-coloured chestnut husks.
Carved angels blow kisses.
A blue teddy sits on a bed of pine needles.
A cloud spills diamonds from its velvet purse.

Bouquets surround the coffin trolley wheels;
The widow's tears fall by her children's heels.
The salesman smile attempts to cheer the plaque
That bears his name. Cause of death: heart attack.
Here I am, Lord, sopranos from on high;
The speeches make me want to cry.
Onyx necklace, the limousines and hearse
Adorn rush hour. I hear he wrote some verse.
The mouth of death opens for its capsule:
Swallows it whole, so natural, so cool.

My eyes well up with tears I cannot cry;
My body is alive but wants to die.
Sunlight dapples the leaves on Orwell Road;
No time today to decipher this code.
Wives in alloy wheel jeeps drop kids to school;
Sometimes you have to be kind to be cruel.
Politicians vomit words in the Dáil;
The willow weeps, a freeze-frame waterfall.
I want the world to stop so I can rest;
Who said life should be a prolonged stress-test?

I thank you, eyes, for showing me this stage –
The haze of flies above a dead cat's guts;
Dawn seeping into day's blank page;
The sun's death by a thousand cuts.
The dance of light and dark, of sweet and sour;
Silk clouds ribboned by the moon's scimitar;
Neon reflections in Hong Kong harbour;
The roar of laughter from the crowded bar.
The urge to reproduce, to find a mate;
To save coloured paper; accumulate.

Thank you, eyes, for showing me fireworks:
Aquamarine, viridian and rose –
The comet's pendant on velvet;
Eiffel tower in fog toga.
My son bemused at entering this world;
Snow silently layering Phoenix Park.
The clouds' make-up when sun tangents the sea:
Lavender eye-liner and apricot blusher.
Thunder-split clouds, fearsome downpour;
Moss-packaged rocks, rinsed by the Owendoher.

Thank you daisy chain spiral galaxies
For brightening my way, Charolais cows
For ear-flicking and tail-whisking as you
Bow to absorb your greens. Thank you, hedgerows
Half-sprayed with white, blossom-bedecked
Wide chestnut trees that guard contented lambs,
Luminous clouds for boldly shadowing
The freshly lacquered gorse and buttercups.
Lastly, you men in yellow hats, for earth
Moving, for steam-rolling tarmac: *Well done*.

Thank you, dear heart, for pushing fluid through my veins,
For keeping the currency of my cells circulating.

For waging implacable war against bacteria.
For patching me up when I cut myself:
For being there beneath chest skin and hair.
You never missed a beat. Always on time,
Miraculously parting my red sea,
Then flooding me with deepest sympathy.

I thank you, brain, for doing my thinking for me,
For acting as head office to my bodily activity.
You never lost the head: it is fitting that you receive
This small token on behalf of the firm,
A gold-plated walnut, which I am sure you will treasure.

I thank you, lungs, for enduring years of abuse:
When I filled you with yellow tar
In street café and sleazy nightclub bar.
When I forced you to wear nicotine's noose.
You never groaned at this indignity,
But just kept working at your steady pace
With tolerance and calm maturity.
You ignored others and ran your own race.
You have been an inspiration to me.
A real breath of fresh air. Would you agree?

I thank you, nose, for making scents for me:
Mist-shrouded pine forest, new paperbacks,
Cut grass, cordite, seaweed, salt air and sand.
For nappy sniff and talcum powder whiff,
For lavender, the bees' metropolis.
Thank you for reddening in cold weather,
For sourcing me so many asteroids.
We've faced life together.
How could I cut you off,
At this, my final hour?

I thank you, legs, for standing up for me
When run to ground despite blister and bruise:
For taking me around Belfast city
In my brand new Brooks running shoes.
Thank you for marching me across the square,
For getting me home drunk at break of day:
For putting the boot in for me those rare
Moments when I had no choice but to stay.
Don't take your foot off the pedal just yet!
Enjoy your winner's lap without regret.

I thank you, ears, for hearing out life's symphony
For listening to squeaky clean fresh snow
Being imprinted by my Wellingtons;
For honest-to-God Gregorian chant,
Car horn morse code, whipcrack and tiger pant.
For fireworks' starburst, for midnight hoots,
Carillon chimes in stereo,
Toast somersault and beaver grunts.
Now that you are laid low, close to the ground,
Please wake me when you hear the trumpet sound.

I thank all you who died that I might live:
You fields of barley, wheat and rice,
You mud-daubed potatoes, you granny smiths,
You Jaffa oranges, you brave salmon,
You silent lambs, you grape clusters.
My body is composed of all of you:
And I thank you for being part of me.
I leave my last remains to you, O Lord.
Hard to believe the world is about to
Have its first day in my absence.

Other Irish Poets from Anvil

MARTINA EVANS

All Alcoholics Are Charmers
Can Dentists Be Trusted?
Facing the Public

'Martina Evans's poems are a miracle, for the way they combine total clarity with profundity: the way the apparently innocent and observant humour of their narrative surface covers a compassion and understanding that are often heartbreaking and heartbroken.'

BERNARD O'DONOGHUE

THOMAS McCARTHY

The Non-Aligned Storyteller
Mr Dineen's Careful Parade
Merchant Prince
The Last Geraldine Officer

'Not many poets have the gift of being able to write so tenderly about private affections and so acutely about public figures and events.'

BRENDAN KENNELLY

DENNIS O'DRISCOLL

Long Story Short
Weather Permitting
Exemplary Damages
New and Selected Poems
Reality Check

'It is as a poet of European temperament, and stature, that O'Driscoll demands to be judged. His terrain is, in effect, without borders: mordant, open, sharp, generous, and sad.'

GEORGE SZIRTES

www.anvilpresspoetry.com